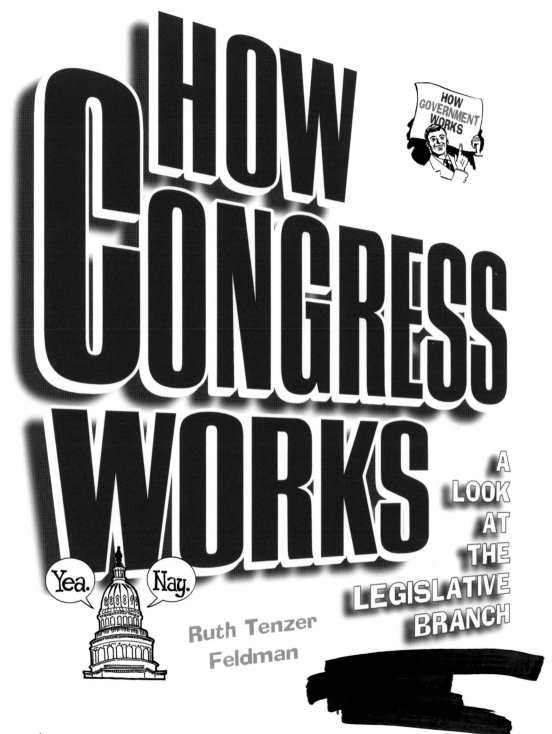

HOW CONGRESS WORKS

HOW GOVERNMENT WORKS

A LOOK AT THE LEGISLATIVE BRANCH

Yea. Nay.

Ruth Tenzer Feldman

LERNER PUBLICATIONS COMPANY • MINNEAPOLIS

For Kate and Amy

With thanks to Roger Marcotte, Systems Administrator for Congresswoman Constance Morella, and Elizabeth Roach, Director of the Senate Page School.

Lerner Publications Company
A division of Lerner Publishing Group
241 First Avenue North
Minneapolis, MN 55401 U.S.A.

Website address: www.lernerbooks.com

Library of Congress Cataloging-in-Publication Data

Feldman, Ruth Tenzer.
　　　How Congress works: a look at the legislative branch / by Ruth T. Feldman.
　　　　　p.　　cm. — (How government works)
　　　Summary: Explores the establishment and history of the U.S. Congress,
　　its organization, duties, and limits, and a typical day for its members.
　　　Includes bibliographical references and index.
　　　ISBN: 0-8225-1347-1 (lib. bdg. : alk. paper)
　　　1. United States Congress—Juvenile literature. [1. United States. Congress.]
　　I. Title. II. Series.
　　JK1025.F45　2004
　　328.73—dc21　　　　　　　　　　　　　　　　　　2003001626

Manufactured in the United States of America
1 2 3 4 5 6 – DP – 09 08 07 06 05 04

TABLE OF CONTENTS

INTRODUCTION:
BUILDING A DEMOCRACY

QUICK QUESTION: Why do we have a Congress? If you're scratching your head, you're not alone. The answer to this question involves some history.

(Above) In 1773 colonists protested high British taxes on tea and other everyday items. Disguised as Native Americans, some of the colonists dumped a shipment of tea into Boston Harbor.

The word *congress* comes from Latin words meaning "to come together." In the eighteenth century, that's exactly what some angry American colonists did. Great Britain ruled the American colonies. The colonists came together because they thought Britain was treating them very unfairly. They believed that if they were united and spoke together, they'd have a more powerful voice.

But King George III of Great Britain didn't listen to the colonists. So they took a drastic step. In 1776 they acted together again and declared a War of Independence against Great Britain. They won, and in 1783 the colonies became the United States of America.

What then? After all the problems with Great Britain, Americans were suspicious of government. The new

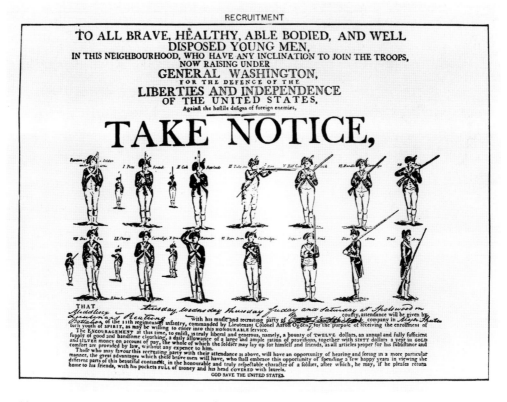

This poster calls on able-bodied American colonists to fight for independence from Great Britain.

states wanted to be free to do things their own way. But they also knew they needed to stick together. The American people wanted to be united, but they didn't want a government that could do whatever it chose without listening to its citizens.

In 1787 representatives from each state got together and wrote the Constitution of the United States. The Constitution explains the purpose of the federal (central) government and how it should work. It wasn't easy to hammer out the details of this new Constitution. It had to work for everyone, and not everyone wanted the same thing. But everyone soon agreed that the federal government would have three separate branches—executive (the president), legislative (Congress), and judicial (the courts). The Constitution spelled out what each branch could and couldn't do. The branches would have to work with each other so that no one branch would become too powerful.

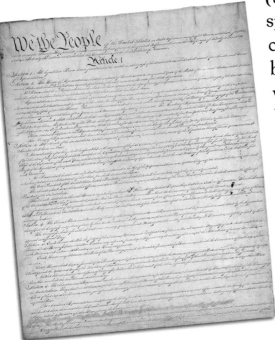

The original Constitution of the United States is on display in the National Archives Building in Washington, D.C.

The first article (part) of the Constitution describes the Congress, or legislature, of the United States. A legislature is a group of elected people who make laws. The U.S. Congress is divided into two parts, the House of Representatives (House) and the Senate. Members of the House are usually known as representatives and serve two-year terms. Members of the Senate—senators—serve six-year terms.

CONGRESS UNDER THE CONSTITUTION

The first federal Congress began in 1789 and ended in 1791. Members did a lot of work. They added a Bill of Rights to the new Constitution. They set up departments in the new federal government. They organized the postal system and made laws to raise money. Members also created a system of courts. They even established a permanent home for Congress, the Capitol, and created the District of Columbia (Washington, D.C.).

Did You KNOW? The Capitol was built at the top of Jenkins' Hill in the new city of Washington. People began referring to the activities of Congress as happening on "the Hill."

Members of Congress have been working hard ever since. This book will tell you how the men and women elected to Congress do their jobs. Maybe after reading this book, you'll want to be a senator or representative!

Washington, D.C., in 1834

Chapter 1
THE POWERS OF CONGRESS

QUICK QUESTION: Congress has the power to a) fire the school principal, b) capture pirates, c) make all dogs wear shoes, or d) none of the above. Would you believe it's "b"? Punishing pirates for "felonies committed on the high seas" is one of the powers of Congress listed in the U.S. Constitution. Members of Congress don't really worry about pirates much anymore, but they have a lot of other powers.

Congress ended many pirating careers. It has the power to punish people for crimes committed at sea.

Before we understand how Congress works, we have to understand what the Constitution requires and allows Congress to do. The Constitution includes some very specific powers for Congress. They include collecting taxes, minting (making) new coins, establishing post offices, and regulating business with other countries. All lawmaking powers belong to Congress too. Making laws is the main way Congress carries out its responsibilities and does its part to make our government work.

But the framers (original writers) of the Constitution also knew they couldn't think of every decision Congress would have to make. So they included some powers that aren't so specific. For example, Congress must "provide for the common defense and general welfare of the United States." This means Congress must always consider the well-being of citizens. So Congress has the power to make decisions about education, health care, and other important issues.

The framers also included what's called the "elastic clause." This clause *stretches* the power of Congress to

Congress created the U.S. Mint in 1792. These women are checking the weight of new coins at the U.S. Mint in Philadelphia, Pennsylvania, in the early 1800s.

make all laws "necessary and proper" for carrying out government duties under the Constitution. The elastic clause has been used for things like creating a federal banking system and setting up the U.S. Air Force.

Orville Wright *(right)* and U.S. military personnel inspect one of the first Wright Brothers' planes in 1908. Congress did not use the elastic clause of the Constitution to create an air force until 1947.

Congress also has power over how the government spends money. Members of Congress work together and with the president to come up with programs to help people and businesses. Then Congress passes a law to set up a program and decides how much money the federal government should spend on it. After deciding an amount, Congress passes a law to set aside that money just for that program.

MORE THAN LAWMAKERS

Congress does more than make laws. Congress has the power to oversee government activities and to investigate, or study, how well laws are working. Let's look at one example of Congress using its investigative power. In August 2000, the Firestone Company announced that it had made mistakes in manufacturing some of its tires. Millions of those tires were already on people's cars and

This sport utility vehicle (SUV) was involved in a two-car accident. Firestone tires are believed to have caused the accident.

sport utility vehicles (SUVs). The tires were thought to have caused accidents and crashes. Why weren't any manufacturing problems with the tires caught earlier? Congress asked officials in the U.S. Department of Transportation and others to look into the question and report back. As a result of the report, Congress passed the TREAD Act. This law requires manufacturers to improve tire safety.

Congress also has the power to declare war. Since 1789 Congress has declared war only five times. But thousands of American soldiers have fought in many conflicts, including wars in Korea, Vietnam, and Iraq. That's because the president is the commander in chief of our military forces. The president can send U.S. soldiers to fight in major conflicts without a formal war declaration from Congress.

The Constitution also gives Congress the power of impeachment. Impeachment means charging a public official (such as the president or a judge) with a crime. The Constitution divides impeachment powers between the House of Representatives and the Senate. The House can charge a public official with a crime, if a majority votes to do so. The Senate then has the power to put the official on trial. If the official is found guilty, he or she can be forced to leave office.

The Constitution grants some powers only to the House or only to the Senate. All bills (ideas for laws) for raising money start in the House. The House also has the power to choose the president of the United States if no presidential candidate wins a majority of the votes cast by the Electoral College, a group of people selected from each state. The Senate can approve or reject treaties (agreements) the president makes with other countries. The Senate also has the power to approve or reject people the president wants to appoint to certain positions, such as Supreme Court justices (judges).

Finally, Congress has the power to propose changes to the Constitution. Two-thirds of the members of the House and Senate must pass a bill proposing a Constitutional amendment (change). The bill is then sent to

President Jimmy Carter (left) shakes hands with General Omar Torrijos of Panama (right) after signing the 1977 Panama Canal Treaty.

state legislatures. Three-fourths of all the state legislatures must approve the bill before it becomes an amendment.

We know what the Constitution says about the powers of Congress. But how does Congress get the job done? Let's find out.

CHAPTER 2
LIFE UNDER THE CAPITOL DOME

TRUE OR FALSE? Senators and representatives are elected by voters. The answer is True. American voters choose some members of Congress on Election Day—the first Tuesday in November of every even-numbered year. Once elected, each new Congress begins at noon on January 3 of the next year and lasts for two years. Every two years a new Congress begins. It's

The Capitol's 287-foot dome is one of the most famous sights in the United States. Builders began work on the dome in 1856. In 1863, the last part of the dome, the 19-foot *Statue of Freedom*, was lifted to its place at the very top.

considered new because some of the members are new. The first year of a Congress is called the first session. The second year is—no surprise!—the second session.

The House and Senate don't meet every day during these sessions. During an average two-year Congress, the Senate meets about 384 days. The House meets a few days less.

Did You KNOW? We number Congresses every two years from the first federal Congress to the present. The Congress that started in 2003 was the 108th Congress.

OPEN FOR BUSINESS

Formal meetings of the House and Senate are called legislative days. A legislative day begins with an opening call to order. It lasts until there is an adjournment (a formal end to the meeting). Sometimes legislative days last for several calendar days. If opening call was three days ago and there still hasn't been an adjournment, it's the same legislative day. So it can be April 25 inside the House or Senate and April 28 on the street outside!

DIG DEEPER What happens if a member can't finish his or her term? The Constitution provides that the state's governor can call an election to replace the member. The governor can also appoint someone to fill the position until the next election.

Members take a break during the day's work by declaring a recess. A recess is usually called at the end of a workday, too, if the legislative day hasn't adjourned. Before recess or adjournment, members decide when they'll return to work. But at the end of a session (year), members usually don't set a specific time to return. This is called an adjournment sine die. That Latin phrase means "without a day." If members adjourn without setting a specific time to return, the next session automatically begins on January 3.

WORK, WORK, WORK

Members of Congress have a lot to do in a short time. Let's do the math.

During the 106th Congress (1999–2000), members considered a total of about nine thousand bills. They passed only about six hundred of those bills into law. Each bill had an average of twenty pages. That's 180,000 pages of material to study. If members worked only during the days Congress was in session, they would each have to read about 470 pages a day! All this reading is in addition to overseeing and investigating how the government is being run.

DIG DEEPER What if something important happens after Congress leaves for the year? Our Constitution gives the president the power to call Congress back into a special session after an adjournment sine die.

How do members do it all? They work hard. When in session, senators and representatives work about eleven hours a day. When they are not working in Washington, D.C., members work in their home state or district. They meet with their

Was someone from Congress too busy reading to notice they were posing for this statue?

constituents—voters in their state or district.

Members have organizations to help them with their work. The Library of Congress (the government's main library) prepares about one thousand law, business, and history reports every year for Congress. The library also answers more than 500,000 research questions a year from senators and repre-

THE LIBRARY OF CONGRESS

The Library of Congress is the oldest federal institution in the United States and the largest library in the world. The library has about 530 miles of bookshelves containing more than 18 million books, 2.5 million recordings, 12 million photographs, 4.5 million maps, and 54 million manuscripts.

sentatives. The Congressional Budget Office prepares studies of taxes and government spending and estimates how much each proposed law would cost. The General Accounting Office reports on the economy and on how well government programs are working.

Every day that Congress is in session, members also use the Government Printing Office (GPO). The GPO publishes the *Congressional Record*, a journal of all discussions and speeches from the House and Senate. The GPO also publishes other reports and documents for Congress.

Members also rely on staff workers and aides. Staff workers and aides help members read through bills. They do research and write reports. They also run members' offices in Washington, D.C., and in their home state or district. College students and other volunteers help too. And the House and Senate have special messengers, called pages, who help keep track of all the documents.

Paging through Congress

Eric Ode says that watching Congress at work is "way better than TV." Michelle Rappaport agrees with him. Eric and Michelle know what they're talking about. They were Senate pages. They spent nearly six months in 2002 working from a platform in the middle of the Senate. You can hardly get closer to Congress than that!

Congressional pages are young people who deliver packages, take messages, and get materials ready for members of Congress. About one hundred pages worked with Eric and Michelle. They were all high school juniors, at least sixteen years old.

Each page has an elected sponsor in the House or Senate. Usually pages come from the same state as their sponsors. Eric comes from Burlington, Vermont. His sponsor was Vermont senator Patrick Leahy, a Democrat. Michelle comes from Salt Lake City, Utah. Her sponsor was Utah senator Orrin Hatch, a Republican.

Michelle Rappaport *(left)* and Eric Ode *(right)*

Pages go to school in Washington, D.C. They start school at 6:15 A.M. and have classes until about 9:45 A.M. Then they report for work. They stay on duty in Congress as long as the members are formally meeting—sometimes way past midnight!

Many other workers help out in the Capitol, where there are places to eat, exercise, get a haircut, mail packages, and cash checks. Doctors and other medical services are available. There's even a subway that runs between the Capitol and several buildings. You could spend days in Congress without ever going outside!

COMMITTEES TO THE RESCUE

Members divide their duties among committees. That way each member does not have to become an expert on everything. Committee members work as a team to study issues and prepare solutions. Congressional committees are very important. A committee is the first place a new law begins to take shape.

Committees handle big topics. Smaller committees, called subcommittees, study specific issues in more detail. For example, the House Committee on Agriculture includes a subcommittee on special crops (such as honey and peanuts) and another on livestock (farm animals).

Standing, or permanent, committees in the House and Senate are the backbone of Congress. These committees study and discuss important issues such as health, education, and the environment. They also usually control which bills will be voted on in the House and Senate.

> **PEOPLE FILE** In 1968 California senator George Murphy moved to a desk in the back row of the Senate. Senator Murphy loved candy and always kept a drawer full of it. Murphy invited everyone to share the treats. That desk in the back row is still known as the candy desk. Every senator who sits there makes sure plenty of mints, hard candies, and chocolates are on hand. Candy manufacturers supply the candy for free.

SENATE BEAN SOUP

There are several stories about how Senate Bean Soup became famous. The most well-known story comes not from the Senate but from the House of Representatives. One day in 1904, so they say, Representative Joseph Cannon sat down for lunch in a restaurant in the Capitol. He looked over the menu but did not see bean soup listed.

"Thunderation," he cried. "I had my mouth set for bean soup! From now on, hot or cold, rain, snow, or shine, I want it on the menu every day."

Senate bean soup has been on the menu ever since.

> 2 pounds dried navy pea beans
> 4 quarts hot water
> 1½ pounds smoked ham hocks
> 1 onion, chopped
> 2 tablespoons butter
> salt and pepper to taste

Wash the beans and run hot water over them until they are slightly whitened. Place beans in a pot with the hot water. Add ham hocks and boil slowly, covered, for three hours. Remove the ham hocks and set aside. When the ham hocks are cool enough to touch, pull the meat off the bones, dice it, and return it to the soup. In a skillet, lightly brown the chopped onion in butter and add to the soup. Before serving, bring soup to a boil, then season with salt and pepper.

Serves 8

The House and Senate usually have separate committees. But when Congress is working on a bill, representatives and senators also meet together on conference committees. Conference committees discuss different versions of a bill that House and Senate members have passed separately. They write one final version of the bill that both the House and Senate will vote on.

Joint committees also include both representatives and senators. The oldest is the Joint Committee on the Library, started in 1800. This committee makes sure the Library of Congress has the money and resources it needs.

The House or Senate can also establish a select, or temporary, committee for a specific purpose. Select committees choose a specific topic to investigate. For example, a Select Committee on Homeland Security was formed after the September 11, 2001, terrorist attacks in New York and Washington, D.C. That committee oversees the creation of new laws to help prevent future terrorist attacks.

Almost everything that Congress does, large and small, starts with a committee. It's important for senators and representatives to get involved in committee work

LEARN THE LINGO

Ever see senators' or representatives' names on a TV screen or in the newspaper? Did you wonder what the letters after their names mean? The letters stand for their political party and their home state. So Senator Richard Shelby, a Republican from Alabama, would be Sen. Richard Shelby (R-AL). Representative Tammy Baldwin, a Democrat from Wisconsin, would be Rep. Tammy Baldwin (D-WI).

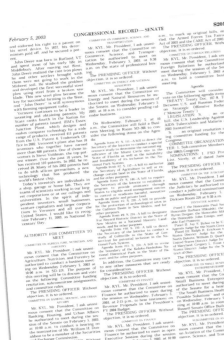

On this page of the *Congressional Record*, February 5, 2003, Senator Jon Kyl (R-AZ) asks for senators' full agreement to schedule meetings of several committees.

that serves the interests of constituents (voters). For example, if you are a senator from a state where many people make their living from farming, you will probably want to join the Agriculture Committee.

The leaders of the House and Senate decide who serves on which committee. But members let leaders know which committees they'd prefer. Members usually serve on two or three committees and on several subcommittees.

Most committee leaders come from the majority party. For example, if sixty Democrats and forty Republicans are elected to the Senate, the Democrats are the majority party in the Senate. They would lead the Senate and chair (run) the Senate committees. The Republicans, in this case, would be the minority party.

Some members don't belong to a major political party. They are Independents or members of a smaller party such as the Green Party. Democrat or Republican members invite them to participate on committees too.

CHAPTER 3
OUR HOUSE

QUICK QUESTION: Do you like the first day of a new school year? OK, it's not as good as summer vacation, but it can be fun.

Opening day of a new Congress at the House of Representatives is pretty fun too. Hundreds of people from all over the United States come to celebrate. The House chamber and visitors' gallery are

In an opening day tradition, House minority leader Nancy Pelosi (D-CA) passes the official gavel to Dennis Hastert (R-IL) *(right)*, the Speaker (chief officer) of the House.

GET COUNTED!

California is a large state with a big population, so in the 107th Congress (2001–2002) it had the most representatives—52. Next was New York, with 31 representatives, and then Texas, with 30. Seven states—Alaska, Delaware, Montana, North Dakota, South Dakota, Vermont, and Wyoming—had only one representative, due to small populations.

So how does the government know how many people live in each state? The Constitution requires the federal government to take a census every ten years to count everyone in the country. The Census Bureau mails a form to every home. Residents fill out information (such as their name, age, and race) and mail the census form back. In some cases, census takers walk from house to house collecting information. Beginning in 2000, people could also use the Internet to respond.

packed with representatives and their families and friends. The noise and excitement sound like democracy—government by the people. And that's exactly what the framers of the Constitution intended the House of Representatives to be.

Voters from each state elect a certain number of representatives to office. The number of representatives is based on how many people live in that state. Every state gets at least one representative, no matter how few people live there. Each state is divided into regions called congressional districts. Each district gets one representative. The framers of the Constitution intended each representative to have a small number of constituents.

Originally, the Constitution said each state should have one representative for about every 30,000 people. As our population grew, so did the number of representatives. The House got too big to manage. In 1911 Congress

Joseph Rainey *(above)* from South Carolina was the first African American representative. He was elected in 1870. Jeanette Rankin *(left)* was the first woman elected to Congress. She became a representative from Montana in 1917, three years before women had the right to vote in federal elections.

passed a law that 435 were the most representatives the House could have.

As our population grows, states make their congressional districts larger. The average district has more than 647,000 people. If we had kept to the framers' original formula of one House member for every 30,000 people, we would have nearly 9,400 representatives!

Representatives are elected every two years. At election time, candidates for the House must

1. Be at least twenty-five years old,
2. Be a U.S. citizen for at least seven years, and
3. Live in the state where their congressional district is located (they don't have to live in the district).

RULES RULE!

With so many people in the House, who's in charge? The most powerful leader of the House is the Speaker of the House. The majority party elects this officer to the position. A Speaker usually votes only to break ties. But the Speaker has a lot of other duties. The Speaker decides what business the representatives will discuss on the House floor. The Speaker meets regularly with committee members and influences what happens in their committees. He or she also meets regularly with Senate leaders and with the president. The Speaker represents the House at official government ceremonies and meets with visiting foreign politicians. And the Speaker must meet with his or her own constituents. Because the Speaker is so busy, he or she can appoint another House member to preside (lead) for a short time.

"SOUND BYTE" "They call me Speaker, but they probably ought to call me the listener because I just do a lot of it."
—*Speaker of the House Dennis Hastert (R-IL), 2001*

The second most powerful person in the House is the majority leader, who is also elected by the majority party. The minority party elects a minority leader. Majority and minority leaders have helpers called whips. The whips and their assistants share information about bills with their party members. They also gather together members when an important vote is coming up on the House floor.

The clerk of the House helps with day-to-day operations, including the recording of votes. The sergeant at arms helps the Speaker keep order in the House during debates and voting. House members elect these officers.

Did You KNOW? The term *whip* comes from the British term *whippers-in*, meaning the man who keeps the dogs in line during a foxhunt.

House rules help lawmakers conduct daily business in an orderly way. During the opening day of a new Congress, representatives decide on a set of rules that will govern the House for the next two years. The House Committee on Rules also creates specific rules for every major bill. These rules include time limits for how long members can debate a bill on the floor and rules for the kinds of changes that will be allowed on a bill.

GETTING DOWN TO BUSINESS

The business day officially starts on the floor of the House at about noon. But members are often in their offices long before that. When it is time for members to go to the House chamber, bells ring in the Capitol and the House office buildings.

Most representatives don't have assigned seats in the House chamber. There's a large aisle running down the center of the chamber. Democrats sit on the east side of

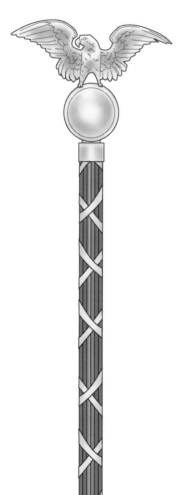

the aisle. Republicans sit on the west side. Independents and members of other parties can sit on either side. The Speaker of the House and several other officers sit up front on a platform.

The Speaker starts the day's session by calling the House to order. Then the sergeant at arms places the mace—a symbol of authority—on the pedestal near the Speaker's platform. The House chaplain usually says a prayer. Representatives say the Pledge of Allegiance and approve the *House Journal* (a written record of the previous day's activities). The Speaker also

The mace (*above*) in the House of Representatives is not just for decoration. In early Congresses, the sergeant at arms would restore order by holding the mace in front of an unruly member.

allows one-minute speeches by representatives on any topic. Then the House gets down to business.

Representatives stand and ask the Speaker for permission to speak. During debates over a bill, the Speaker does not always grant permission. If a representative has already spoken several times, the Speaker may want to give someone else a chance.

When it comes to voting on a bill, representatives often simply call out "yea" (yes) or "nay" (no). The Speaker or presiding officer judges whether there were more yeas or more nays. This is called a voice vote. At other times, representatives vote using one of the House's electronic voting machines placed throughout the House.

HOUSE WORK

All tax and other revenue (money) bills start in the House. Appropriations (spending) bills also start in the House.

The House has the power to decide who will be president if no one wins a majority of votes in an

The House Ways and Means Committee of the First Session, 102nd Congress, is ready to get to work. The committee is in charge of budgets and funding.

They tax our wives, they tax our homes
They even tax our mutts
They're taxing everything we own
No wonder men go nuts!

C-116

Bills about taxes start in the House. Many cartoons make fun of taxes. In this cartoon from the 1930s, the taxpayer at the front of the line is complaining that there's a tax on his wife, his home, and even his dog.

election. In this case, each state gets one vote, no matter how many representatives that state has.

Finally, only the House can begin impeachment proceedings against a president, federal judges, and other federal officers. The House charges the official with "treason, bribery, or other high crimes and misdemeanors." These impeachment charges are then sent to the Senate for a trial.

Did You KNOW? House members have chosen our president twice—Thomas Jefferson in 1800 and John Quincy Adams in 1824. In 1876 the House created a special commission to determine which votes to accept in the election between Rutherford B. Hayes and Samuel J. Tilden. Hayes won.

CHAPTER 4
OUR SENATE

QUICK QUESTION: Did you know ancient Rome had a senate too? In many ways, the Roman Senate was different from the modern U.S. Senate. For one thing, U.S. senators don't have to wear special shoes and purple-striped robes called togas! But the Romans had some very important ideas. They believed that a country's laws should be discussed and voted on by wise people. The framers of the Constitution wanted our Senate to also be a place where wise people spend time discussing laws and deciding what's best for the nation.

HOW THE SENATE IS ELECTED

The Constitution created the Senate to be more stable than the House of Representatives. For that reason,

Roman senators (*above*) gathered in the forum (public place) to discuss laws and government as U.S. senators do in Congress.

senators are elected for six-year terms. Only one-third of the members of the Senate runs for office in each election.

So, for each Congress, two-thirds of the Senate are returning members. In the House, the entire membership is newly elected with each new Congress. Senate rules and procedures are in effect all the time. They do not have to be voted on at the beginning of every new Congress, as rules and procedures in the House do.

Senators have not always been directly elected (elected by the people). Before 1914 members of state legislatures chose their senators. The Constitution was changed in 1913 to provide for direct election of senators.

Every state elects two senators, no matter how small the state is. That means Congress has one hundred senators. At election time, Senate candidates must

1. Be at least thirty years old,
2. Be a U.S. citizen for at least nine years, and
3. Live in the state from which they are elected.

Cooperation Counts

Like the House, the Senate has powerful leaders. But Senate leaders rely less on rules and more on the cooperation of every senator.

The Constitution names the vice president of the United States as president of the Senate. But he or she can only vote to break a tie. So the vice president doesn't preside very often, except when an important vote or a special ceremony takes place in the Senate.

When the vice president is absent, the president pro tempore runs the Senate. This Latin phrase means president "for a time." Senators select the president pro tempore. He or she is usually a long-serving member of the majority party. A presiding officer also conducts votes, debates, and other Senate business. Sometimes the president pro tempore takes over the presiding officer's duties.

Did You KNOW? Our first vice president, John Adams, cast twenty-nine tie-breaking votes in the Senate. That record still stands. At least eleven vice presidents have not had a single chance to break a tie vote.

The Senate has majority and minority leaders too, who are elected from the largest and second largest parties. They are assisted by majority and minority whips.

The secretary of the Senate is in charge of a lot of the day-to-day business. Among other things, he or she keeps public records of Senate business, supervises the Senate pages, and makes sure there are enough computers, papers, and pens. The Senate has a sergeant at arms to maintain order and ensure security. The secretary and sergeant at arms are nonpartisan employees, meaning they work for all senators, not just for those in one political party.

A Day in the Senate

Like the House, the Senate begins its business day around noon. Senators take their seats at individual desks that are assigned to them. Senate pages have already piled the desks with bills, reports, and other paperwork.

Democrats sit on the west side of the main aisle of the chamber. Republicans sit across the main aisle on the east side of the chamber. Independents and members of other parties are assigned seats based on seniority and other factors. The presiding officer and several other leaders sit in the front of the chamber.

After the opening bell, the presiding officer calls the Senate to order. The chaplain leads a prayer, and the senators say the Pledge of Allegiance. The *Senate Journal,* a log of the previous day's activities, is read out loud and approved. The secretary also reads out loud any messages from the president, the House of Representatives, or the majority or minority leader of the Senate. Messages may be about any upcoming bills or other Senate business.

The Senate of the 107th Congress

Every day in session, senators receive two calendars. These aren't calendars the way we usually think of them. The calendar of business—also called the legislative calendar—contains information on bills and resolutions (formal opinions). The executive calendar contains information about treaties and nominations. It's called the executive calendar because treaties and nominations come from the president, the head of the executive branch. The calendars only show what may be discussed. Congressional schedules list what the Senate intends to discuss on a particular day.

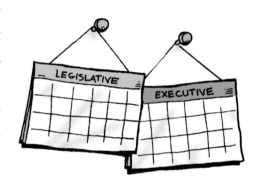

Two special calendars, the legislative calendar and the executive calendar, influence senators' schedules.

The Senate often works out details of a bill on the floor. Senators can debate a bill for a long time and offer amendments on any subject. Unless everyone agrees to put a time limit on discussion of a bill, a debate can go on for hours and even days.

During a debate or discussion, if a senator wants to speak, he or she has to stand and address the presiding officer. The senator can't say anything until the presiding officer allows it. But the presiding officer must recognize (call on) the senator who addressed the officer first. Senators can't interrupt each other in a debate without first being recognized by the presiding officer. But a senator who "has the floor" (has the right to speak) may allow another senator to say something brief or to ask a question. That's called yielding. During a debate, if a senator is rude or does not follow the rules, the presiding officer can call that senator to order. That's a little like a time-out! The senator has to sit and be quiet for a while.

FILIBUSTERS

Every senator has the power to filibuster a bill. To filibuster means to delay or prevent a vote by talking for as long as necessary. Senators filibuster when they are really against a bill but do not have enough votes from other senators to defeat it. During a filibuster, a senator does not have to stick to the topic of the bill. He or she can talk about anything. In the 1930s, Louisiana senator Huey Long filibustered by reciting famous plays or reading recipes out loud.

Senator Huey Long (D-LA) chose interesting material for his filibusters.

Strom Thurmond (1902–2003) was the oldest and longest continuously serving member of Congress. Thurmond was a senator from South Carolina for eight terms, from 1954 to 2002.

The longest filibuster in Senate history happened in 1957. To stall a vote on a civil rights bill, Senator Strom Thurmond of South Carolina spoke for twenty-four hours and eighteen minutes.

Often just the threat of a filibuster helps senators work out a compromise. Under Senate rules, the filibuster ends if at least three-fifths of the Senate votes for cloture. Cloture limits further debate on the bill and forces senators to vote.

Senators cannot cast electronic votes. Most votes are taken by simply calling for yeas and nays. Otherwise, the Senate uses a roll-call vote. Each senator's name is read aloud, and that senator answers with his or her vote.

SENATE POWERS

The Senate has the power to approve or reject certain decisions the president makes. For example, the Constitution states that the president must get at least two-thirds of the Senate to approve any treaty (agreement) with another country. The Senate also has to agree to the president's

President Ronald Reagan wanted Sandra Day O'Connor to serve on the Supreme Court. The Senate approved, and O'Connor became the first woman justice on the Supreme Court.

choice of some federal officials. These officials include Supreme Court justices and the top leaders of federal agencies. Senators might hold hearings and do a background check on the president's nominee (choice). A two-thirds yes vote approves the nomination.

The House and the Senate share impeachment powers. The House brings charges against a federal official, such as a judge or even the president. The Senate holds the trial and decides if the person is guilty of "treason, bribery, and other high crimes and misdemeanors." The chief justice of the Supreme Court presides over the trial. At least two-thirds of the Senate must vote "guilty" to convict the official.

The Senate has convicted several judges and removed them from office. But impeachment of a president is rare. President Andrew Johnson was impeached and tried in 1868, and President Bill Clinton was impeached and tried

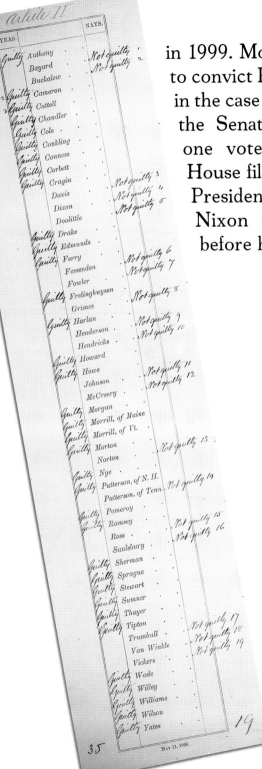

in 1999. Most senators voted not to convict President Clinton. But in the case of President Johnson, the Senate was short by only one vote! In July 1972, the House filed charges to impeach President Richard Nixon, but Nixon resigned from office before his Senate trial.

Senators' votes for or against impeaching President Andrew Johnson were recorded by hand.

CHAPTER 5
CONGRESS AND YOU

TRUE OR FALSE? Once elected, a member of Congress doesn't really worry about what's happening outside of Washington, D.C. The answer is False. When Eric Ode was a Senate page in 2002, he worked for Senator Patrick Leahy of

Members of Congress depend on votes from their constituents. A young person (above) practices voting on a sample ballot.

Vermont. But Senator Leahy also worked for Eric. Eric is from Vermont, and Senator Leahy was elected to serve the people of his home state. Senator Leahy worked for you, too, no matter where in the United States you live.

SERVING THE CITIZENS

Members of Congress care about what we have to say. They learn about our views directly through our letters, e-mails, and phone calls. Members spend time in their home states and districts talking to constituents. They also learn about what's on our mind through public opinion polls. And the Internet and radio and television talk shows let members know what people from all over the country are thinking. But balancing the needs and interests of all people in a democracy can be tough.

Plenty of people—even the president—want to tell Congress what to do. We are all part of this democracy.

In 1922, 87-year-old Rebecca Latimer Felton (D-GA) filled the vacancy caused by another senator's death. She served for just twenty-four hours, but she was ready to take phone calls from constituents.

WRITE A LETTER TO CONGRESS!

You don't have to travel to Washington, D.C., to meet your representative or senators. Members have offices in their home states. Contact them before you plan a visit to make sure they'll be available.

You can also e-mail or call. The House of Representatives' website <www.house.gov> and the Senate's website <www.senate.gov> list members and contact information. You can also get information from your local library, the local chapter of the League of Women Voters, or your local newspaper. Some telephone books also list senators and representatives in a U. S. government section.

It's often more effective to write a letter. The address for a senator is

The Honorable [senator's full name]
United States Senate
Washington, D.C. 20510

The address for a representative is

The Honorable [representative's full name]
United States House of Representatives
Washington, D.C. 20515

Start your letter to a senator with, "Dear Senator [senator's last name]. Start your letter to a representative with, "Dear Mr. or Ms. (or Representative, Congressman, or Congresswoman) [representative's last name]. Tell them clearly who you are and what information you'd like. Tell them what school you go to and be sure to include a return address.

Since the first Congresses, groups of people have gotten together to pressure Congress on issues they are interested in, such as slavery, taxes, health care, and extending the right to vote to women. But how much influence over Congress should one group of people have? That's a difficult question.

LOBBIES

Some organizations send representatives to Washington, D.C., to talk to lawmakers about certain issues. The organizations are called lobbies, and their representatives are called lobbyists. Lobbyists give members of Congress facts and information they hope will make the members vote in favor of their issues. Doctors have lobbyists working on health care and insurance issues. Farmers have lobbyists working on agricultural issues. Oil companies have lobbyists working on foreign trade issues. Hundreds

Suffragists (women lobbying for women's right to vote) present their arguments to the House Judiciary Committee.

of lobbyists work with Congress to make laws that are favorable to the people they represent.

It's a crime for members of Congress—or any government officials—to ask for or take money or gifts in exchange for voting or acting in a certain way. Members and lobbyists have gotten in trouble over that. And some people think lobbyists have too much influence in Congress, even if they're not doing anything wrong. But most lobbyist practices are perfectly legal and protected by the Constitution.

This political cartoon criticizes the Senate for allowing in powerful lobbies. The giant lobbyists represent wealthy monopolies (big businesses), such as coal, steel, and oil, that are trying to control what the Senate does.

Young people line up to attend a 2001 Senate hearing about Napster, a popular Internet music-sharing service. They want to show senators that they support Napster.

LET THE SUNSHINE IN

Congress works mostly indoors, but Congress is also referred to as "government in the sunshine." This means that you can see or find out most of what Congress does. The House and Senate chambers have visitors' galleries, where you can see the action taking place on the floor. The public is also allowed in most committee hearings.

Congressional debates are printed every day in the *Congressional Record*. The *Record* is sold to the public and available on the Internet. Debates and votes are also televised on the C-SPAN TV channels. Many newspapers, magazines, TV programs, and websites discuss what's happening in Congress.

In 1995 Congress started its own site on the World Wide Web, at http://thomas.loc.gov. Known as *Thomas,* the site got its name from President Thomas Jefferson. The Library of Congress puts a ton of information on *Thomas,* including every amendment to every bill. The House and Senate have sites too. Members have home pages on the Web. What's happening in Congress is just a mouse click away.

Congress's website, http://thomas.loc.gov, is called *Thomas* to honor President Thomas Jefferson.

EXPECT CHANGE

The Constitution gave us a general outline for how Congress works. But many details have changed as the needs of the nation have changed. Members of Congress are free to rewrite the rules by which they work on bills, establish committees, conduct investigations, and do other activities. Voters are also free to amend our Constitution, as we have done in the past.

Michelle Rappaport was a Senate page in the 107th Congress (2001–2002). She wants to be a senator one day. In 2015 she will be thirty years old—the minimum age for Senate candidates. The first Congress she could serve in would be the 115th Congress, which begins in 2017.

One thing is certain. The 115th Congress will be different from the 107th Congress. If she is elected, Michelle would join a Senate that probably has more women and more minorities.

What other changes will Michelle find in the 115th Congress? In part, that depends on you. You can decide what you want to change in our nation and which members of Congress to contact to help make those changes happen. You can make a difference even if you are not yet old enough to vote. Congress belongs to all of us. Michelle put it this way: "A nine-year-old could write a letter and it could end up on the desk of every senator on the Senate floor."

Even if you don't yet have a vote, you have a voice. Use it!

It's easy to write a letter to someone in Congress.

THE LIFE OF A BILL

1) IDEA

2) SUPPORT

3) INTEREST GROUP

7) THE COMMITTEE
STUDIES THE BILL

8) THE BILL GOES ON
A CALENDAR

9) CONSIDERATION
BY THE HOUSE

13) THE BILL GOES BACK
TO THE FULL SENATE

14) CONFERENCE
COMMITTEE ACTION

15) THE BILL IS PRINTED

4) LOBBY CONGRESSPERSON

5) BILL INTRODUCED IN THE HOUSE

6) BILL ASSIGNED TO COMMITTEE

10) INTRODUCTION IN THE SENATE

11) ASSIGNMENT TO A SENATE COMMITTEE

12) COMMITTEE ACTION

16) VOTED UPON IN HOUSE AND SENATE

17) THE SPEAKER OF THE HOUSE AND VICE PRESIDENT SIGN BILL

18) THE PRESIDENT SIGNS OR VETOES (REJECTS)

CAPITOL COMPLEX MAP

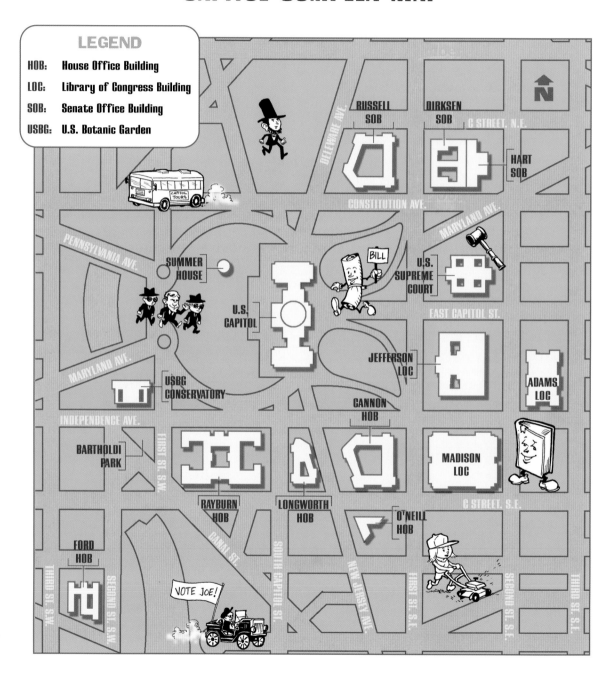

LEGEND

HOB: House Office Building
LOC: Library of Congress Building
SOB: Senate Office Building
USBG: U.S. Botanic Garden

GLOSSARY

adjournment: an action ending a legislative day

adjournment sine die: an action to end a session of Congress without setting a new date to meet again. Sine die is Latin for "without a day."

bill: proposed law

chamber: legislative body in Congress, the Senate or the House of Representatives

Congress: the legislative (lawmaking) branch of the U.S. government

constituent: a person represented in Congress by an elected official. Residents of a state are that state senator's constituents. Residents of a congressional district are that district representative's constituents.

filibuster: a tactic to delay voting on a bill, in which a senator speaks for as long as necessary

hearing: a formal meeting, usually held by a committee of Congress, in which members of the public present their views on bills or on topics of interest to Congress

House of Representatives (House): a chamber of Congress in which the number of voting members is based on the population of each state

law: a bill that has passed both houses of Congress and has been signed by the president or otherwise authorized to take effect

legislative day: a formal meeting of the House or the Senate that begins with the call to order and ends with adjournment

member: a person who is part of the House of Representatives or the Senate and who is allowed to vote on the House or Senate floor

recess: interruption in the meeting session

Senate: a chamber of Congress in which there are two voting members from each state

veto: the power of the president to refuse to approve a bill passed by Congress

SOURCE NOTES

For quoted material: pp. 9, 10, 11, the U.S. Constitution, art. I, sec. 8, at http://memory.loc.gov/const/const.html, accessed June 24, 2003; p. 18, Eric Odeand Michelle Rappaport, interview with the author, Washington, D.C., June 4, 2002; p. 20, recipe from the U.S. Senate website at http://www.senate.gov/reference/reference_item/bean_soup.htm, accessed June 25, 2003; p. 26, Dennis Hastert quoted in Kathy Kiely, "'Listener' of the House Takes Reins," *USA Today,* June 8, 2001, page A.11; pp. 30, 38, the U.S. Constitution, art. I, sec. 8, at http://memory.loc.gov/const/const.html, accessed June 24, 2003; p. 47, Rappaport.

BIBLIOGRAPHY

Bickford, Charlene Bangs, and Kenneth R. Bowling. *Birth of the Nation: The First Federal Congress 1789–1791.* Landham, MD: Madison House Publishers, 2002

Commanger, Henry Steele, ed. *Documents of American History.* 7th ed. New York: Appleton-Century-Crofts, 1963.

Davidson, Roger H., and Walter J. Oleszek. *Congress and Its Members.* Washington, D.C.: CQ Press, 2002.

The Original U.S. Congress Handbook, 107th Cong., 2nd sess., 2002. State edition, edited by Amy K. Mitchell. Washington, D.C.: Votenet Solutions, Inc., 2002.

Smith, Steven S. *The American Congress.* 2nd ed. New York: Houghton Mifflin Company, 1999.

U.S. Government Printing Office. *Our American Government.* Washington, D.C.: GPO, 2000. H. Doc. 106–216.

Wolfensberger, Donald R. *Congress & the People: Deliberative Democracy on Trial.* Washington, D.C.: The Woodrow Wilson Center Press, 2000.

FURTHER READING AND WEBSITES

The Architect of the Capitol
<http://www.aoc.gov>
Learn why the Capitol's location was chosen and how the Capitol was designed and constructed. See the Capitol grounds, office buildings where your senators and representatives work, the Supreme Court Building, and the U.S. Botanic Garden Conservatory.

"The Branches of Government," *Cobblestone Magazine,* January 2003.

Donovan, Sandy. *Making Laws: A Look at How a Bill Becomes a Law*
Minneapolis: Lerner Publications Company, 2004.

Jones, Veda Boyd. *The Senate*. Philadelphia: Chelsea House Publishers, 2000.

Kowalski, Kathiann M. *A Balancing Act: A Look at Checks and Balances.*
Minneapolis: Lerner Publications Company, 2004.

League of Women Voters
<www.lwv.org>
The League of Women Voters was founded in 1920 on the idea that Americans
should know for whom and what they're voting. The website provides information
on the election process, people running for office, and current issues. There is also
a directory for finding information on your senators and representatives.

The Library of Congress
<http://www.loc.gov> or <http://thomas.loc.gov>
Learn about the library's collections of books, maps, and photographs. Plan a visit.
Or "Jump Back in Time" to another era in American history, "Meet Amazing
Americans" from Thomas Jefferson to King Kamehameha I of Hawaii. Listen to
audio interviews about historical and current events. Link to *Thomas,* an Internet
library designed to make information about Congress easily available to the public.

The Office of the Clerk of the U.S. House of Representatives
<http://clerkkids.house.gov>
Check out "Kids in the House," an interactive center. Write a simulated bill
online, use the Learning Center resources, and test your knowledge of Capitol
trivia.

Partner, Daniel. *The House of Representatives*. Philadelphia: Chelsea House
Publishers, 2000.

United States Senate
<http://www.senate.gov>
Find your state senators, take a virtual tour of the Capitol, and learn about the art
and history of the senate chamber.

United States House of Representatives
<http://www.house.gov>
Find your district's congressional representative, learn what bills are currently
being discussed on the House floor, and find links to other websites detailing the
legislative process.

INDEX

ABOUT THE AUTHOR

Ruth Tenzer Feldman has written several books related to U.S. history and government. She has drafted education bills proposed by Presidents Reagan, (George H. W.) Bush, and Clinton, and learned firsthand how Congress works from her experiences as a legislative attorney in the U.S. Department of Education. Feldman is also a regular contributor to *Cobblestone* and *Odyssey* magazines, and her work has been published in the United States, Canada, and France. She lives with her family in Bethesda, Maryland.

PHOTO ACKNOWLEDGMENTS

The photographs in this book are reproduced with the permission of: © CORBIS, pp. 4, 10; National Archives, p. 5, 6, 39; Historic Urban Plans/Smithsonian Institution, p. 8; © The Granger Collection, New York, p. 9; Air Force, p. 11; © CORBIS/SYGMA, p. 12; Carter Library, p. 13; © A. A. M. Van der Heyden/IPS, p. 14, 16; © Ruth Tenzer Feldman, p. 18; courtesy of the Government Printing Office, p. 22; © Reuters NewMedia/CORBIS, p. 23, 37; University of Montana, Mansfield Library, p. 25 (left); Library of Congress, pp. 25 (right) (LC-BH832-769), 28 (LC-USZC4-4293), 41 (LC-USZ62-68544), p. 43 (LC-USZ62-2023), p. 44 (LC-USZ62-9678); © Lake County Museum/CORBIS, p. 30; © Scala/Art Resource, NY, p. 31; © U.S. Senate Photo Studio, p. 34; © IPS, p. 36; Ronald Reagan Library, p. 38; © Jim West, p. 40; © Mario Tama/Zuma Press, p. 45; © Todd Strand/IPS, p. 47. The diagram on p. 7, the illustrations on pp. 26, 35, and 46, and the map on p. 50 are by Bill Hauser.